I0818461

My Mom's full name

Date of birth

Place of birth

My Mom's mother's full name

Date of birth

Place of birth

My Mom's father's full name

Date of birth

Place of birth

Mom, your life is a gift.

You hold within you a story that only you can share. Use these pages to fill with your one-of-a-kind memories—whether it's a special moment from your childhood, an unforgettable adventure, or a piece of advice to share. Speak from the heart, in your own words—it doesn't need to be formal or complex. Because when you are finished, you will create a gift that will be loved for generations.

CHILDHOOD *home*

What was your home like growing up? Include details like the neighborhood, who lived with you, what your room was like, and how and where your family spent time together.

We do not remember days, we remember moments.

Cesare Pavese

TRADITIONS

Your favorite holiday growing up was:

Some family holiday traditions were:

Memorable gifts (big or small) you received were:

Family RELATIONSHIPS

What was your relationship like with your parents?

Did you have special relationships with any other family members?

Being A KID

What do you miss most about being a kid? It could be a specific activity or perhaps a feeling you miss.

...childhood
lasts all
through life.

Gaston Bachelard

NOTABLE

Nicknames you've had...

Name:

Where it came from:

Name:

Where it came from:

Names of pets you've had:

Names of childhood friends:

What were your friends like?

First MEMORIES

What is your earliest memory?

When you were little, how would you get to school?

As a child, you were afraid of:

Your favorite toys were:

You've always had a natural talent for:

Some of the chores you had growing up were:

What was your first paying job, and how much were you paid?

Where are some interesting places you've visited?

What made them so memorable?

Today I know that
such memories are
the key not to the past,
but to the future.

Corrie Ten Boom

What are one or two things you did that you never told your parents about?

What rules did your parents have, and which ones did you test the most?

TRAVEL

If you could go back in time to relive any moment in your life, what would it be? And why?

...history
isn't just the past.
It's alive in us.

Natalie Portman

SCHOOL *days*

Names of schools you attended:

Your favorite subjects in school:

Do you remember any favorite teachers? What were their names, and why were they special?

What did you want to be when you grew up? (And it could be multiple things.)

Favorite childhood books:

Favorite childhood TV shows:

Favorite childhood music:

Favorite childhood games or sports:

Favorite childhood hobbies, interests, or collections:

What was it like to become a mother?

What are some of your very first memories of your children?

A mother is
the one who fills
your heart in
the first place.

Amy Tan

FAMILY *traits*

Ways your children are like you or their other parent:

What are some of your favorite things you've done with your children?

The most precious thing a parent can give a child is a lifetime of happy memories.

Frank Tyger

MOMENTS OF *laughter*

List 5 memories of when your children were young that still make you laugh:

SIGNS OF *affection*

How do you show your love to your children? Do you shower them with gifts? Praise their successes? Maybe you gently encourage them to do their best or have a special tradition just between you. Share them here:

By giving children
lots of affection, you can
help fill them with love
and acceptance
of themselves...

Wayne Dyer

WORDS TO *remember*

Things you've often said to your kids:

Things your children have said that you'll never forget:

Role MODELS

Who are some people you admire and why? These could be lifelong friends, celebrities, family members, etc.

RESEMBLANCE

What are some ways you are like your parents? How are you different?

The best thing
to hold onto in life
is each other.

Audrey Hepburn

YOUR *favorites*

One of your favorite colors is:

Most days, you're wearing:

Your favorite dessert is:

A smell that makes you stop every time is:

You love playing this game:

A book that has stuck with you is:

Music you love to listen to is:

Your favorite movie of all time is:

You're happiest when you are:

YOUR BEST *qualities*

What are some things people often compliment you on?

Which one means the most to you and why?

What about you has stayed the same throughout your life? What's changed?

[Kids] don't
remember what
you try to teach them.
They remember
what you are.

Jim Henson

Three THINGS

3 things you're proud of:

3 things you're passionate about:

3 things you've lost:

3 things you look forward to:

Life MOTTO

What is your favorite quote or saying? Or maybe you have several? Share them here and describe what they mean to you.

LIFE *lessons*

What is one of the toughest lessons you've learned in life?

How has it changed you (for better or worse)?

Other things
may change us,
but we start and
end with family.

Anthony Brandt

LIVED

List the places that you've lived in throughout your life:

What would you like to do in your lifetime?

While we try
to teach our children
all about life, our
children teach us what
life is all about.

Angela Schwindt

World EVENTS

Significant events you've seen in your life...

Event:

When it happened:

Where you were:

How it affected you:

Event:

When it happened:

Where you were:

How it affected you:

Event:

When it happened:

Where you were:

How it affected you:

THE BEST OF *motherhood*

What's the biggest challenge about being a mother?

What's the best thing about being a mother?

...there are only two lasting bequests we can hope to give our children. One of these... is roots, the other, wings.

Hodding Carter

Sound ADVICE

If you could pass along one piece of advice, what would you say?

A LASTING *wish*

What wishes do you have for your children?

When you look at your life, the greatest happinesses are family happinesses.

Joyce Brothers

Written by: Miriam Hathaway

Designed by: Steve Potter

Edited by: Amelia Riedler and Bailey Vega

ISBN: 978-1-970147-80-3

© 2023 by Compendium, Inc. All rights reserved. No part of this publication may be reproduced or transmitted in any form or by any means, electronic or mechanical, including photocopy, recording, or any storage and retrieval system now known or to be invented without written permission from the publisher. Contact: Compendium, Inc., 1420 80th Street SW, Suite C, Everett, WA 98203. *My Mom: In Her Own Words*; Compendium; live inspired; and the format, design, layout, and coloring used in this book are trademarks and/or trade dress of Compendium, Inc. This book may be ordered directly from the publisher, but please try your local bookstore first. Call us at 800.91.IDEAS, or check out our full line of inspiring products at live-inspired.com.

4th printing. Printed in China with soy inks on FSC®-Mix certified paper.

Create meaningful moments with gifts that inspire.

CONNECT WITH US

live-inspired.com | sayhello@compendiuminc.com

@compendiumliveinspired
#compendiumliveinspired